# 2 Women 1 God

## On the road to Redemption

Leah Joslyn

2 Women 1 God Copyright 2020© Leah Joslyn

All rights reserved. No part of this book may be reproduced or transmitted in any form, without the written permission of the author, except for brief quotations for review purposes.

Scripture quotations taken from the (NASB®) New American Standard Bible®, Copyright © 1960, 1971, 1977, 1995, 2020 by The Lockman Foundation. Used by permission. All rights reserved. www.lockman.org

Published by ELOHAI International Publishing & Media:
P.O. Box 1883
Cypress, Texas 77410
elohaipublishing.com

ISBN: 978-1-953535-18-4


Printed in the United States of America

# Woman of Promise

Who is a woman of promise? A woman of promise walks in victory, she doesn't fight for victory, but from victory. She realizes that she has already overcome, and her past no longer affects her future negatively. What matters most is now — what she is going to believe now. She understands that God has not given her a spirit of fear, but of power, love, and a sound mind. She is confident of who she is in Christ and she cannot be shaken. She believes that she is all that God has called her to be; she is a woman of promise.

# Contents

Week 1 . . . . . . . . . . . . . . . . . . . . . . 7
Viewer Guide . . . . . . . . . . . . . . . 8
Prayer Points . . . . . . . . . . . . . . . 10
Ruth 1:1-5 . . . . . . . . . . . . . . . . . . 11
Questions . . . . . . . . . . . . . . . . . . 16

Week 2 . . . . . . . . . . . . . . . . . . . . . 21
Viewer Guide . . . . . . . . . . . . . . . 22
Prayer Points . . . . . . . . . . . . . . . 24
Ruth 1:6-13 . . . . . . . . . . . . . . . . . 25
Questions . . . . . . . . . . . . . . . . . . 30

Week 3 . . . . . . . . . . . . . . . . . . . . . 33
Viewer Guide . . . . . . . . . . . . . . . 34
Prayer Points . . . . . . . . . . . . . . . 35
Ruth 1:14-22 . . . . . . . . . . . . . . . . 37
Questions . . . . . . . . . . . . . . . . . . 41
Ruth 2 . . . . . . . . . . . . . . . . . . . . . 43
Questions . . . . . . . . . . . . . . . . . . 48

Week 4 . . . . . . . . . . . . . . . . . . . . . 51
Viewer Guide . . . . . . . . . . . . . . . 52
Prayer Points . . . . . . . . . . . . . . . 53
Ruth 2:10-23 . . . . . . . . . . . . . . . . 55
Questions . . . . . . . . . . . . . . . . . . 59

Week 5 . . . . . . . . . . . . . . . . . . . . . 63
Viewer Guide . . . . . . . . . . . . . . . 64
Prayer Points . . . . . . . . . . . . . . . 65
Ruth 3 . . . . . . . . . . . . . . . . . . . . . 67
Questions . . . . . . . . . . . . . . . . . . 72

Week 6 . . . . . . . . . . . . . . . . . . . . . 77
Viewer Guide . . . . . . . . . . . . . . . 78
Prayer Points . . . . . . . . . . . . . . . 79
Ruth 4 . . . . . . . . . . . . . . . . . . . . . 81

Viewer's Guide Answers . . . 88
Beloved Poem . . . . . . . . . . . . . . 89
About the Author . . . . . . . . . . . 90

# Introduction

Everyone has their own redemption story. They just don't know it yet! I believe that, sooner or later, everyone will experience something devastating and shocking, but in the midst of their hopelessness, they will experience God up close and personal. We each have to make the choice to believe that God is who He says He is and to accept His redemption for us.

# Viewer guide – Session One

Ruth 1:1-7

Today's session will introduce us to the Historical background of the book of Ruth.

After Moses delivers the children of Israel out of Egypt, God promises to take them to the _____ _____ called CANAAN.
After Moses' death, the mantel is passed on to Joshua and he prepares the children of Israel to cross the Jordan river and enter into the promise land. They go over the promises of God- the _____ _____ and also the _____ of God- what would become their _____ if they disobeyed.

Deuteronomy 29:29 (write out below)
_____
_____
_____

Deuteronomy 30:1-3 (write out below)
_____
_____
_____

Deuteronomy 31:20 (write out below)
_____
_____
_____

LESSON #1 PROJECTED _____ VS _____.

Joshua 23:7-8, 12 (write out below) _____
_____
_____
_____
_____
_____

Many of the Tribes failed to completely drive out all their _____.
God then had to raise up _____ to deliver the people.

LESSON #2 STOP _____ WITH THE _____.

These are the JUDGES that God raised up: Othniel, EHUD, Deborah, Gideon, (Abimelech Gideon's son usurped for three years); Tola, Jephthah and Samson.

So our story focuses on _____ the Judge as it pertains to Ruth.

The children of Israel suffered from INCONSISTENCY and _____.

CONSEQUENCE #1 – There is a _____ in the land.

CONSEQUENCE #2 – God sends King _____ of Moab to take control of Israel.

Israel serves Eglon of Moab for ___ years. (Judges 3:14)

LESSON #3 – PROMISE _____ vs _____ LAND.

TERRITORY _____ can become TERRITORY _____.

LESSON #4 – DON'T MAKE MAJOR _____ WHEN IN A _____.

LESSON #5 – WHOSE VOICE ARE YOU _____ TOO?

# Prayer Points

- Is the any area of my life that seems like a famine because of disobedience?

- Is there any area of my life where I am not walking by faith but by sight?

- Are there any voices that I am listening too, instead of your voice?

- Are there personal choices that I may be making that may be negatively influencing others?

# Ruth 1

**Ruth 1:1-5 NASB**

1 Now it came about in the days when the judges governed, that there was a famine in the land. And a certain man of Bethlehem in Judah went to sojourn in the land of Moab with his wife and his two sons. 2 The name of the man was Elimelech, and the name of his wife, Naomi; and the names of his two sons were Mahlon and Chilion, Ephrathites of Bethlehem in Judah. Now they entered the land of Moab and remained there. 3 Then Elimelech, Naomi's husband, died; and she was left with her two sons. 4 They took for themselves Moabite women as wives; the name of the one was Orpah and the name of the other Ruth. And they lived there about ten years. 5 Then both Mahlon and Chilion also died, and the woman was bereft of her two children and her husband.

As we begin this study of Ruth, I think it is important for us to know a bit of the background and history of the characters. So we begin with Elimelech and his wife Naomi. As we see in verse one, they lived in the country of Canaan, the promised land given to the children of Israel since the time of Moses and Joshua. Remember, after the Lord rescued the children of Israel out of Egypt under the leadership of Moses, He led them through the desert for forty years. Then, finally, under the leadership of Joshua, they crossed the river Jordan and after a series of battles, they conquered the land of Canaan. This land was the land that God promised to Abraham, Isaac, and Jacob. Deuteronomy 31:20 (NLT) says, "For I will bring them into the land that I swore to give their ancestors — a land flowing with milk and honey. There they will become prosperous, eat all the food they want, and become fat…" Elimelech and Naomi were also Ephrathites from Bethlehem in Judah.

Verse one tells us that a famine struck the land of Canaan. Commentaries would say that it was due to an invasion in the land, but what is certain is that this was a problem not just for Elimelech and his family but for everyone. In life it is guaranteed that problems will come in all forms. The question is how are we going to respond to them? So as we continue to read, in verse two we see that Elimelech's response to the problem was to leave Canaan, the promised land, and go to Moab, a fruitful land.

### What is the history of Moab?

Do you remember that in Genesis 13, both Abram and Lot were travelling together, but all their flocks together became too many, and disputes broke out amongst their people so Abram suggested to Lot that they separate? Lot looked around and chose the fertile plains of the Jordan Valley. Sometime afterwards, Lot had to be rescued from war and he ended up settling in Sodom and Gomorrah, two cities which were filled with so much wickedness that God had to come down and see for Himself what was really going on, eventually destroying them. Only Lot and his two daughters survived the tragedy and they went to live in the mountains. His two daughters were concerned that they would not be able to have offsprings since there were no men nearby, so they got their father drunk and committed incest with him (Genesis 19:36). One gave birth to a son called Moab of whom came the Moabites, and the other gave birth to Ben-ammi of whom came the Ammonites. The Moabites were idolatrous people who worshipped their gods, Chemosh and Baal-Peor, and participated in human sacrifices.

The saga continues in Numbers 25 where the men of Israel began to have sexual relations with the women of Moab who also invited them to attend their sacrifices to their gods. The men feasted and worshipped with them, resulting in the Lord becoming angry and sending a plague amongst His people resulting in the death of 24,000 people.

We can see that Moab had very sinful roots, but somehow Elimelech saw that the land looked green and fertile and decided to move his family there. Just like Lot, the father of Moab, he looked with his physical eyes to determine what would be best for his family. As the saying goes, the grass always looks greener on the other side, especially when you are going through a famine or have a problem in your life. So where does a child of Israel, who lived in the Promised land go for refuge? To Moab because it appeared fruitful.

I guess some of us are just throwing up our hands saying, "Yeah Elimelech you were just plain dumb! How could you leave the land God gave to you along with all His promises and go to Moab expecting to find respite (a break from a difficult situation)?" Maybe some of us are also saying, "Yeah, it's not so bad, what was he supposed to do? Stay and starve?" Either way I believe he should have never left where God had placed them, where God's presence dwelled (the Ark of the Covenant was there) to find comfort elsewhere regardless of the famine. I believe that here lies a warning for us today, that we should never seek comfort outside of the presence of God and His people, regardless of the situations we are facing. The world does not have the solutions or the answers to our problems. It does not have the truth. It might seem like the world will be more accepting of us when we leave God's protection, and that we might become more fruitful, but my friend it will only end in greater loss. Better to be in a famine with the Lord, better to be under His discipline than in the world, away from Him, living in circumstances which seem more favorable.

By the end of verse three, we see that Elimelech dies, he never gets a chance to repent and go back to Canaan. Something that was supposed to be temporary became permanent. His widowed wife and sons become even more desperate and the two sons marry Moabite women. Elimelech's poor choice to move to Moab temporarily results in a worse choice: the marriage of his sons to Moabite women. These men marry women who come from a tribe which is idolatrous and displeases God. They go right back to what God had delivered them from. Ten years pass, ten years of continued separation and disobedience, then Naomi's two sons die. Now Naomi has nothing left except her two daughters-in-law, who are Moabites.

This is how it all begins, we say to ourselves that we are just going to make a little compromise over here, just take a little break from this hard situation. We seek respite somewhere outside the boundaries of God, and then one thing leads to the next and before we know it, we have found ourselves in the whirlwind of a mess. Surely, this was not the end that we were hoping for. Surely, we didn't think that things would have escalated to that. What is really unfortunate is some of us never get the chance to repent and turn back to God like Elimelech and his two sons. It was too late for them, for they had died in their separation from God, in their disobedience, in their sins. James 1:15 NLT says, "when sin is allowed to grow, it gives birth to death.

**The world does not have the solution or answers to our problems.**

# Questions
Ruth 1:1-5

1) What famine(s) have you gone through or are you going through in your life?

2) What land looks greener to you?

3) What is Moab in your life?

4) What are the idols you have started to worship?

5) How have you justified your sins? What excuses have you told yourself and others for your poor choices?

6) What have been the consequences? _____

_____
_____
_____
_____


7) What is keeping you away from turning to the Lord? What are some lies you have believed from the enemy or doubts and fears that you have?

_____
_____
_____
_____

# Additional Insights

# Additional Insights

# Additional Insights

# Viewer guide – Session Two

Ruth 1:1-5, 6-13

Today's session will highlight how the children of Israel defeated some of their enemies, restored fellowship with God, and brought an end to the famine in the land.

Elimelech and his family were _____ of Bethlehem in Judah. The ancient name of Bethlehem in Judah in Jacob's time was Eph'ratah. (Genesis 35:16)
Eph'ratah was part of the land that belonged to the Tribe of _____.
E'phrath or Eph'ratah means _____ or fruitful.

The Levite priest cuts his wife into _____ pieces and sends it to all the twelve _____ of Israel. (Judges 19:29)

The Israelites went to seek God at _____.
- The first time he told them to go, the Benjamites killed _____,000 Israelites.
- They sought God again a second time and he told them to go fight. But the Benjamites defeated _____,000 Israelites.
- They sought God a third time and He told them to go fight the Benjamites. That day thirty Israelites were killed. But they slaughtered 100 Benjamite swordsmen. Then 18,000, 5,000 and 2,000. God gave them the victory. The Tribe of Benjamin lost 25,000 men and only 600 men survived because they escaped to the rock of _____ where they lived for four months. (Judges 20:48)

LESSON #6 - DELAYED _____ IS NOT A _____ FROM GOD.

LESSON #7 - A SMALL _____ CAN LEAD TO A GREATER _____.

After Israel's repentance in Judges 3, God raises up _____ who is a Benjamite.

After the death of King _____, the _____ ends.

**LESSON #8** - GOD WANTS TO _____ THOSE _____ _____ IN YOUR LIFE.

**LESSON #9** - DO NOT _____ YOUR HEART AGAINST GOD.

**LESSON #10** - HEALING AND DELIVERANCE IS A _____ AND REQUIRES _____, _____ AND _____.

**LESSON #11** - YOU CANNOT _____ ALL OF THE CONSEQUENCES.

**LESSON #12** - WHO ARE YOU _____?

# Prayer Points

- Are there any areas of your life where you hold resentment towards God?

- Are there any areas of your life where you feel it is impossible for God to fix?

- Ask God this week to show you your weak spots and your blind spots.

- Are there any prayer requests that you believe God is able to fulfill for others but not yourself?

- Ask God to reveal to you why you struggle to trust Him in those specific areas.

**Ruth 1:6-13 NASB**

**6** Then she arose with her daughters-in-law that she might return from the land of Moab, for she had heard in the land of Moab that the Lord had visited His people in giving them food. **7** So she departed from the place where she was, and her two daughters-in-law with her; and they went on the way to return to the land of Judah. **8** And Naomi said to her two daughters-in-law, "Go, return each of you to her mother's house. May the Lord deal kindly with you as you have dealt with the dead and with me. **9** May the Lord grant that you may find rest, each in the house of her husband." Then she kissed them, and they lifted up their voices and wept. **10** And they said to her, "No, but we will surely return with you to your people." **11** But Naomi said, "Return, my daughters. Why should you go with me? Have I yet sons in my womb, that they may be your husbands? **12** Return, my daughters! Go, for I am too old to have a husband. If I said I have hope, if I should even have a husband tonight and also bear sons, **13** would you therefore wait until they were grown? Would you therefore refrain from marrying? No, my daughters; for it is harder for me than for you, for the hand of the Lord has gone forth against me."

In verse six, we read that Naomi hears that the Lord has visited her people and has given them food. Isn't God always faithful to His people? Will He not always provide? He may not always show up at the time that we would like Him to (as in this case more than ten years passed since the time when the famine had started in Israel), but He will always show up. This situation just magnifies how much Naomi had doubted God and His faithfulness towards His children. She is the one that left and walked away from Him and His provision, but now she is going back to Him in all her brokenness. She is defeated and dejected, life has happened to her and she has experienced a lot of death and loss. She has lost her security and her protection. In those days a woman without a man was in a dangerous situation because the husband was the one who provided for her and took care of all of her needs. Naomi and her daughters-in-law needed that headship.

So, Naomi hears what the Lord is doing and her faith is revived. Faith comes by hearing the word of God (Romans 10:17). However, I think that at this point her faith is very small, but it doesn't matter because God can work with anything. She makes an active choice to change her circumstances and her situation. No one can make this choice for you. You have to decide for yourself that you are turning back to the Lord. The good news for us is that the Lord is always there waiting with open arms to receive us. He is waiting to redeem us and our situations. He wants to make provision for the famines in our lives. Isn't that great news? The not so great news is that it is not going to be a walk in the park for us. It is going to take some participation on our part. We have to be willing to work along with God, exercise our faith, and trust Him in order to see change and deliverance. It is not going to be easy and we are going to need some patience.

In verse eight, Naomi says to her two daughters-in-law, "Go back to your mother's house." But if you observe carefully, they had already left where they were. They had already started the journey back to the land of Judah and on the way Naomi tells them to turn back. I must wonder, why in the world would Orpah and Ruth want to go with Naomi? Naturally they would initially want to go because of their relationship, but it is also natural that as soon as they were given the opportunity to return home, where they grew up, where they belonged, with a people, religion, and culture they were accustomed to, they would take it. Instead they refuse the first time, maybe in order to be polite, so Naomi insists further, giving even more explanations. I still wonder if maybe part of them wanted to stay because in the midst of Naomi's disobedience and separation from God, they saw a light, however dim it was. Had they experienced something different that caught their attention in a way that made them want to go with her? Was Naomi thinking that it would be best for them to return so that she wouldn't have to take them to Judah with her? In her mind was she playing out how people would respond when they saw her returning with two women from Moab? Maybe she didn't want the people to see the sin that had happened in her house and she didn't want a reminder of it. No, it would be much easier for them to return to their mothers' houses, that way she could forget about them and all that had happened to her. It would be her little secret. She could just say that her husband and sons died, the end!

I find it interesting that she blesses them saying, "May the Lord be good to you and may he bless you with a husband and security." It seems like she was willing to do anything to convince and persuade them to stay and to let her return alone. Moreover, she blesses them in the name of the Lord whom she no longer believes is going to bless her. She is hoping that they would find blessing in the place where her life was cursed and where everything went downhill, how ironic. I have personally found myself in Naomi's position one too many times. Believing that God is good, but not for me! That God will bless and provide, but just not for me. What is even more interesting is that she prays that God will bless them with husbands. I cannot tell you how many times I have prayed with my friends, that God will bless them with good, excellent husbands, but once again I did not believe that for me! It is easy to believe that there is no hope for us personally, no bright and prosperous future. How many of us have believed God for salvation, but stopped right there? We have not continued to believe Him for the abundant life that He has promised to us! Naomi insists that they must go back because she can do nothing for them; it is too late for her, and she is too old to have another husband.

Some of you are believing a lie that it is too late. Yes, you are going back to God but it is too late for Him to do something great. You believe He can't do much with you, and He can't use you. You have missed the calling on your life; it is too late to find your destiny and purpose. Maybe you have reached middle age or you have some handicap… whatever your situation might be, it is never too late for the Lord to do something. Look at Sarah, who was ninety years old when Isaac was born. Look at Elisabeth, who was advanced in years when she had John the Baptist. It does not matter how long you have been living in sin, how long you have been lukewarm in your faith, how long you have been pretending that you actually know what you believe in, how long you have been struggling, how long you've been drowning, how long you have been lost. Today is the day to be FOUND. It is never too late! And for those of you who are really young and have no idea what I'm talking about, just tell yourself it's never too early. Go tell your parents it's never too early. Tell them that you are going to do all that the Lord has called you to do because you are a woman of promise, then continue reading this book.

Satan also likes to bring up this lie that our situation is the worst and that no one in the world has been through anything as bad as we have, causing us to isolate ourselves from people. Do not fall for it, my friend! Pray that the Lord sends you at least one godly person that can keep you in prayer as you make this journey back to God.

> We have to be willing to work along with God, exercise our faith and trust Him to see change and deliverance.

# Questions
Ruth 1:6-13

1) What areas of your life have you decided to give back to the Lord?

2) What are some potential areas of difficulty that you see ahead? E.g. Resistance from family members, loss of relationships, isolation, rejection.

3) Do you have any hope for complete deliverance or do you have doubts? If so what are they? E.g. I'm too old, I've gone too far etc.

4) Is there anyone that you can trust to accompany you prayerfully during this journey?

# Additional Insights

# Additional Insights

# Viewer Guide – Session Three
Ruth 1:19-22, Ruth 2:1-9

Today's session will focus on Naomi and Ruth's return back to Bethlehem of Judah and Ruth working in Boaz's fields.

LESSON #13 - _____.

SECURITY MEANS - _____, _____, _____, _____.

List 4 ANTONYMS of security - _____, _____, _____, _____.

LESSON #14 – CHOOSE YOUR _____ CAREFULLY.

LESSON #15 – WHAT IS YOUR _____?

STEP 1 – FIND YOUR _____.
STEP 2 – FIND _____.
YOU MUST FIND YOUR _____ FIRST BEFORE FINDING _____.

KINSMAN- "_____ AVENGER" OR "_____" MEANING.
COMING TO _____ OR _____.

LESSON #16 – STAY, _____, _____.

# Prayer Points

- Ask the Lord to show you the things that you are basing your identity on.

- Ask God to show you the lies that you are believing about your identity.

- Ask God to reveal to you the things you are finding security in.

- Ask God to show you why it is difficult to walk in your God-given identity and to accept the security that he has provided to you.

- Ask God to bring to your remembrance the ways in which your words have hindered someone on their journey.

- Ask God to show you ways in which you can be kinder to others that need support.

**Ruth 1:14-22 NASB**

**14** And they lifted up their voices and wept again; and Orpah kissed her mother-in-law, but Ruth clung to her. **15** Then she said, "Behold, your sister-in-law has gone back to her people and her gods; return after your sister-in-law." **16** But Ruth said, "Do not urge me to leave you or turn back from following you; for where you go, I will go, and where you lodge, I will lodge. Your people *shall be* my people, and your God, my God. **17** Where you die, I will die, and there I will be buried. Thus may the Lord do to me, and worse, if *anything but* death parts you and me." **18** When she saw that she was determined to go with her, she said no more to her.

**19** So they both went until they came to Bethlehem. And when they had come to Bethlehem, all the city was stirred because of them, and the women said, "Is this Naomi?" **20** She said to them, "Do not call me Naomi; call me Mara, for the Almighty has dealt very bitterly with me. **21** I went out full, but the Lord has brought me back empty. Why do you call me Naomi, since the Lord has witnessed against me and the Almighty has afflicted me?" **22** So Naomi returned, and with her Ruth the Moabitess, her daughter-in-law, who returned from the land of Moab. And they came to Bethlehem at the beginning of barley harvest.

In verse fourteen, we see that Orpah finally accepts Naomi's counsel, but Ruth does not. In verse fifteen, Naomi tries one last time to convince Ruth to return to her home. She is so engrossed in her own situation and mess that she isn't even immediately aware of the great evangelistic opportunity placed in front of her, where she can influence Ruth to truly come to know God. My friend, evangelization begins at home. Start with the people around you. Sometimes we are so caught up in our own mess and situations that we can hardly see the needs around us. Our visions become blurred. I wonder how many opportunities to be witnesses for Jesus we have missed because we were so caught up in our own problems. I wonder how many times God wanted to use us to reach out to someone, but we refused or didn't even hear Him because we were blinded by our own mess!

In verse sixteen, we are introduced to Ruth and we see how she decides to respond to her situation. First of all, life has been hard to her, and she has experienced loss herself. She has lost her husband; she has no father-in-law, and she is childless after ten years of marriage! Not such a lovely picture—she is three-times cursed! She has no security, no man, and now her mother-in-law wants to get rid of her! What a life. At least if she goes back, she will have some kind of protection which would be better than two women travelling on the road alone. But she insists that no matter the circumstances or the consequences she is going with Naomi. I want to believe that she did not only make this decision because of her loyalty to Naomi even though that may have been part of it. I suspect that in her limited knowledge and understanding, even her limited experience with God, she had tasted something that she could no longer turn away from. I believe that she grew up in a life filled with darkness and idolatry. Yes her homeland was green, but it was only green in appearance. There was no real life and substance to it, but she had seen something through Naomi, the light, the truth, and it was calling out to her. That is what convinced her to go with Naomi despite the old woman's protest against it. She preferred to face the unknown in a strange land with a strange God than to go back to her past life. My friend, suffering under the hand of God is better than owning the riches of the world. As the psalmist said, "Better is one day in your courts than a thousand elsewhere" (Psalm 84:10 NIV). Ruth, in her limited knowledge, understood what was important! Just like Mary, the sister of Martha, in Luke chapter ten.

In verse nineteen, we see that they finally arrive in Bethlehem and the whole city is stirred because of them. The women ask, "Is this Naomi?" And she responds, "No call me Mara for the hand of the Lord is against me." I find it very interesting that Naomi's name means "God is sweet," and Elimelech's name means "God is King." So 'God is sweet' and 'God is King' get married. Then they leave the promised land out of disobedience. Eventually, the one who is called 'God is sweet' returns to the land changing her name to 'bitter' because of how she feels and all that she has experienced. This name change shows us where she is at in her relationship with God. God may be many things, but none of them is bitter! Naomi was bitter because of the consequences of her sins. I can only imagine Naomi and Ruth being the talk of the town and the center of all gossip! You know when you have just come out of sin and you just want to sneak back into the church and not draw too much attention to yourself? You would just like to forget and move on, but NO, everyone is looking at you, talking about you, and asking all sorts of questions. You have repented of your sins and God has forgiven you, but people just can't seem to forget and let it go. So the women asked, "Is it Naomi?" And I am sure that they also asked, "Where is your husband and your two sons, why are they not here with you, and who in the world is this Moabite woman, and why did you bring her with you? Why are you saying that the Lord's hand is against you and that we should call you Mara? Why are you looking tired, worn out, depressed, and hopeless? It seems like you have lost a little weight, what is going on with you?" As women we always have a lot to say especially when someone was in sin and is trying to find their way back to the Lord. I will say nothing further except that each of us should pray and ask the Holy Spirit to convict us of past errors and for future guidance with our words. We should pray that we would actually build up and encourage and not tear down others.

# Questions
Ruth 1:14-22

1) What are some promises from God's Word that you can memorize to solidify your faith in this decision to do whatever it takes to change your situation? Read the following passages: Philippians 2:3, 4:6-7

2) What are your thoughts about God? Are they positive or negative?

3) What beliefs do you have about God's character that are false?

4) What are some promises from God found in the following passages: Psalm 139:17, Jeremiah 29:11, Numbers 23:19, Romans 8:31-39?

_____
_____
_____
_____
_____
_____

5) Have you ever found yourself on the flip side of the coin where you were the one looking and judging someone going through a situation? You were the one gossiping about them? How can you be a positive influence and encouragement to others? What things can you do and say?

_____
_____
_____
_____
_____

# Ruth 2

**Ruth 2:1-9 NASB**

**1** Now Naomi had a kinsman of her husband, a man of great wealth, of the family of Elimelech, whose name was Boaz. **2** And Ruth the Moabitess said to Naomi, "Please let me go to the field and glean among the ears of grain after one in whose sight I may find favor." And she said to her, "Go, my daughter." **3** So she departed and went and gleaned in the field after the reapers; and she happened to come to the portion of the field belonging to Boaz, who was of the family of Elimelech. **4** Now behold, Boaz came from Bethlehem and said to the reapers, "May the Lord be with you." And they said to him, "May the Lord bless you." **5** Then Boaz said to his servant who was in charge of the reapers, "Whose young woman is this?" **6** The servant in charge of the reapers replied, "She is the young Moabite woman who returned with Naomi from the land of Moab. **7** And she said, 'Please let me glean and gather after the reapers among the sheaves.' Thus she came and has remained from the morning until now; she has been sitting in the house for a little while."

**8** Then Boaz said to Ruth, "Listen carefully, my daughter. Do not go to glean in another field; furthermore, do not go on from this one, but stay here with my maids. **9** Let your eyes be on the field which they reap, and go after them. Indeed, I have commanded the servants not to touch you. When you are thirsty, go to the water jars and drink from what the servants draw."

We read in verse two that Ruth decides that she wants to go gleaning because she realizes that they cannot just sit at home doing absolutely nothing forever. It was the time to harvest barley, so this means that it was around April. She asks Naomi to go and glean whatever she can so that they could at least have something to eat. Notice that it was Ruth who wanted to go and who even brought it up, not Naomi. Where did Ruth learn about the law which stated that the leftover grain from the harvest was to be left for the poor and the stranger? Maybe she heard people talking or observed it. This law demonstrated God's love and care for the poor and needy. She saw God's provision for her in the midst of her lack and need. She saw His personal care for her, the Moabitess who was not a child of Israel. God provides for us and He showers his goodness on the just and the unjust (Matthew 5:45).

They were back in the promised land, but work was still required of them. God calls us to participate in His promises. He will not spoon-feed us all of the time. It seems like Naomi is still disconnected from God and His plans for her situation, but Ruth has humbled herself before the Lord hoping to find grace and favour. And so in verse three she 'happens' to end up on Boaz's plot of land. Have you ever just happened to be at the right place at the right time? It is what we call providence and in verse four we continue to see evidence of it. It was that day that Boaz decided to visit his field, suggesting that he didn't go there every day. In fact landowners left their workers in charge of their fields, occasionally dropping in to see how things were going. What a coincidence, the day Boaz stops by is the day Ruth goes gleaning and ends up on his fields.

At the very beginning of this chapter, we are introduced to Boaz, a man of promise, who is another important character in the story. He not only lived in the promised land, but he was also experiencing all of God's promises. There is a difference between being a child of promise and actually living out and experiencing all of the promises that God has for you. You can have salvation, but not be set free. Naomi was also a woman of promise, but she was not enjoying any of its benefits because of her past disobedience. As we continue to look at Boaz, we see that when he first speaks, blessings come from his mouth. He wasn't complaining about his problems or his misery. When you get together with your friends what is the first thing that comes out of your mouth? Also look at the response that his servants give to him. They pronounced blessings on him as well. What is your testimony amongst family, friends and unbelievers? Do they see and experience the goodness of the Lord through you? Or is it mostly, headaches, drama and problems? In verse five, he then asks the overseer of his servants, "Whose young woman is this?" Do you take notice of those who are less fortunate than you are? Do you desire to reach out to the poor, needy, widowed, and orphaned? James 1:27 makes it clear to us that this is what true religion is. In verse seven, the overseer responds stating that she is the young Moabite woman who came back with Naomi and she had asked to stay and work amongst them. I wonder if one of the reasons that Boaz was not judgmental of Ruth was not just because he was a man of good character, but also because of his own background. I find it very interesting that the Lord chose Boaz to be the redeemer (as you will see later on in the story) knowing that his mother was Rahab the prostitute (Joshua 2). She was the one who helped the Israelites escape by letting them down the wall of Jericho when they went to spy out the land. It was her act of courage that saved her and her family from death, and after this she married an Israelite and lived among the Israelites. Maybe Ruth's kindness to Naomi reminded him of his mother's kindness to the men. Maybe he had learned firsthand that God wasn't willing that any should perish, but that all should come to repentance — that it was not one's background and past circumstances that determined who they really were.

Ruth knows that she has to do whatever it takes for her and Naomi to survive. She finds contentment in her situation while still holding on to hope. She does not complain or search for an easy way out. She works with what is available to her. How many times do we find ourselves complaining about our situations instead of making the most out of them? We should be choosing to learn all that we can, 'gleaning' all the truths about God's character and the lessons that He wants to teach us while we are there. The reality is that seasons change, situations change, and there is always something to learn at every stage. In verses 8-9, Boaz gives Ruth instructions which include the words: "stay", "watch", "follow", "do not go!" "Listen carefully, my daughter." God is also asking you to listen to His voice carefully. He wants to speak directly into your situation. So are you ready? You need to humble yourself and go before the Lord and listen to what He has to say. He has specific instructions for each and every one of us:

- **Stay** - stay where He has placed you and stay in the place where you can hear His voice.
- **Watch** - watch how He is directing the situations in your life. Watch where He is leading you. Watch who He is bringing into your life and who He is removing. Watch how He is going to work all things together for your good.
- **Follow** - follow Him, don't hesitate, don't doubt, and don't disobey. Don't follow your friends or Facebook or social media; follow Him alone! At the end of verse nine, there is a promise of protection and provision for Ruth. If you stay, watch, and follow, God will protect and provide for you.

> God calls us to participate in His promises, He will not spoon feed us all of the time.

# Questions
Ruth 2:1-9

1) What things are you finding security in?

2) List some things/situations that cause you to feel a lack of security.

3) Who or what is your identity found in?

4) Explain the connection you see between your identity and your ability to live in security.

# Additional Insights

# Additional Insights

# Viewer Guide – Session Four
Ruth 2: 8-23

This session will examine Ruth's process while working in the fields of Boaz, and God's provision for her and Naomi.

**LESSON #17 - WALK IN _____.**

Keep your _____ on the _____.

**LESSON #18 - WHAT ARE YOU WILLING TO _____?**

**LESSON #19 - LOOK FOR _____!**

**LESSON #20 - GOD WILL GIVE _____ _____.**

**LESSON #21 - BE _____.**

# Prayer Points

- Ask the Lord to show you the people that you can be accountable to.

- Ask God to reveal to you the hidden areas of pride in your life.

- Ask God to help you become aware of the little evidences of his presence in your life.

- Ask God to give you the strength and the motivation to remain persistent in your daily life.

In verse ten, Ruth acknowledges her unworthiness and asks, "Why have I found favour in your sight that you should take notice of me?" Matthew 19:29 says that whoever gives up father, mother, sister, etc. for the Lord's sake shall be blessed. In verse thirteen, Ruth continues by saying, "You have comforted me and spoken very kindly to me." What are our words like? Do we speak comfort and peace when we meet someone who is seeking help? In verse fourteen, Boaz invites her to come and eat with them. Do we include people or exclude them? Do we raise up our hands in condemnation and judgement or do we spread our arms wide open, giving others a warm and loving welcome back? In reality, our words, actions, and responses truly reveal what is in our hearts. So Ruth sits next to reapers and they do not scorn her or curse her. They sit together. If this were our present church context how would we have treated her? Would we have made her sit at the back of the church or excluded her from participating in certain activities? Or would we have welcomed her with open arms and tried to help her as much as possible? Sometimes we want the big jobs, the big positions. We want to be the pastor or the leader of a great flock but are we willing to be faithful in small things? Are we willing to humble ourselves and stoop low to do tasks such as feeding the poor? Are we extending a hand to the needy, or are we too big, high, and mighty for those things? Romans 12:3 tells us that we should not think of ourselves more highly than we ought to, and James 2:1-6 shows us that we should not dishonour the poor.

After Ruth is finished eating, she leaves some for Naomi. She remembers that she isn't the only one in the situation. She thinks of her mother-in-law. As you walk on your journey, what other people does the Lord bring to memory that may be experiencing the same thing as you? Or maybe you have been delivered, so how can you now go back to help someone? She eats until she is satisfied. Satisfaction is something that we are always searching for and usually in all the wrong

**Ruth 2:10-23 NASB**

**10** Then she fell on her face, bowing to the ground and said to him, "Why have I found favor in your sight that you should take notice of me, since I am a foreigner?" **11** Boaz replied to her, "All that you have done for your mother-in-law after the death of your husband has been fully reported to me, and how you left your father and your mother and the land of your birth, and came to a people that you did not previously know. **12** May the Lord reward your work, and your wages be full from the Lord, the God of Israel, under whose wings you have come to seek refuge." **13** Then she said, "I have found favor in your sight, my lord, for you have comforted me and indeed have spoken kindly to your maidservant, though I am not like one of your maidservants."

**14** At mealtime Boaz said to her, "Come here, that you may eat of the bread and dip your piece of bread in the vinegar." So she sat beside the reapers; and he served her roasted grain, and she ate and was satisfied and had some left. **15** When she rose to glean, Boaz commanded his servants, saying, "Let her glean even among the sheaves, and do not insult her. **16** Also you shall purposely pull out for her some grain from the bundles and leave it that she may glean, and do not rebuke her."

**17** So she gleaned in the field until evening. Then she beat out what she had gleaned, and it was about an ephah of barley. **18** She took it up and went into the city, and her mother-in-law saw what she had gleaned. She also took it out and gave Naomi what she had left after she was satisfied. **19** Her mother-in-law then said to her, "Where did you glean today and where did you work? May he who took notice of you be blessed." So she told her mother-in-law with whom she had worked and said, "The name of the man with whom I worked today is Boaz." **20** Naomi said to her daughter-in-law, "May he be blessed of the Lord who has not withdrawn his kindness to the living and to the dead." Again Naomi said to her, "The man is our relative, he is one of our closest relatives." **21** Then Ruth the Moabitess said, "Furthermore, he said to me, 'You should stay close to my servants until they have finished all my harvest.'" **22** Naomi said to Ruth her daughter-in-law, "It is good, my daughter, that you go out with his maids, so that others do not fall upon you in another field." **23** So she stayed close by the maids of Boaz in order to glean until the end of the barley harvest and the wheat harvest. And she lived with her mother-in-law.

places. True satisfaction can only be found in the provision of Jesus Christ. To search elsewhere would only be futile. Psalms 37:4 NLT says, "Take delight in the LORD and he will give you your heart's desires.

In verses 15-16, Boaz changes the rules for Ruth. Not only can she now glean behind the women, but they must now purposely leave out some stalks of grain from the sheaves so that she can collect them. God can cause the rules to change for you! God has a way of giving you blessings that you know you do not deserve. He gave you that job that you were underqualified for, they chose you when others had all their degrees. He gives you favour and sends a complete stranger to open doors for you. He sets you up with all the right connections. You have no right to be in the places that you are and you certainly didn't earn it, but God! He is love and filled with unfailing kindness and goes out of His way to make a way for you. He gives us things that we didn't even know were possible.

In the verses which follow, Ruth returns home and Naomi quickly seeks information from Ruth about the happenings of her day. After listening to Ruth's explanation, in verse twenty Naomi exclaims, "God has not ceased kindness on the living and the dead." The personal hope of Naomi is renewed. Through Ruth's faith and God's intervention, Naomi begins to trust in the Lord again. Sometimes it is your small act of faith that God uses to reach out to someone. Our actions are never in isolation, whether good or bad. Can you imagine what would have happened if Ruth had decided to stay at home with Naomi instead of stepping out in faith, her little faith, to do something risky? Her going out to glean especially as a stranger, a Moabitess, could have resulted in her being (as we see in verses 15, 16 and 22) insulted, rebuked and even assaulted. She risked being abused verbally and physically. But God showed Himself great in her circumstances and because of it Naomi now has hope. In verse twenty-three, we see that Ruth continues to live with her mother-in-law. She continues to remain faithful to the decision she has made. She works during the barley and wheat harvest, which means that she perseveres for months, from the beginning of April to the end of June. So at least three months pass, but she remains faithful. Sometimes we like immediate results, but God cannot be rushed, and we must go through each season. Your faithfulness in each season will determine your growth and advancement. So don't be too eager to change seasons, be like Ruth: **patient, obedient, faithful, and perseverant. Always gleaning!**

# Questions
Ruth 2:1-23

1) What situations are you facing today where God is calling you to step out in faith even though it may seem risky? _____
_____
_____

2) What verses in the Bible can you use to affirm that God can be trusted if you step out in faith and that He will protect you? _____
_____
_____

3) What verses in the Bible show that God's plans for you are good?
_____
_____
_____

4) Are there any specific people in your life that God has brought to you to encourage you in your situations? _____
_____
_____

5) How can you show gratitude to them? _____
_____
_____

6) Have you been an instrument of hope in someone else's life?
_____
_____
_____
_____

7) How can God change your heart towards someone that you have passed by? _____
_____
_____
_____

8) How has God demonstrated His character of love and kindness to you personally? _____
_____
_____
_____

9) List some blessings that God has given to you that you do not deserve:
_____
_____
_____
_____

10) Has God ever failed you or given you reasons to doubt His goodness towards you? _____
_____
_____
_____

# Additional Insights

# Additional Insights

# Viewer Guide – Session Five
Ruth 3:1-18

This session identifies the strategies employed by Ruth and Naomi in order to secure a Kinsman redeemer.

LESSON #22 - GET _____.

Naomi told Ruth that on this particular _____, at this particular _____. Boaz would be at this particular _____, doing a particular _____.

LESSON #21.1- _____ THAT MAN. What are his character traits?

LESSON #22.2 - DISCERN THE _____ _____. There is a favorable time to approach someone.

LESSON #22.3 - _____ YOURSELF. Not just mentally and spiritually but also physically _____ yourself, _____ yourself, _____ yourself and then _____.

LESSON #23 - GET A _____ _____.

LESSON #24 - WHAT IS YOUR _____?

Ruth went down _____ or _____.

LESSON #25 - _____ AND _____.

# Prayer Points

- Ask the Lord to give you a strategy.
- Ask the Lord to reveal any mindsets or attitudes that may be hindering you from finding and implementing a strategy.
- Ask God to reveal to you a strategic counsellor that can offer you wise guidance.
- Ask God to give you the boldness to step out in faith.
- Ask God to give you favor.
- Ask the Lord to reveal to you the areas that you need to work on both inwardly and outwardly.

# Ruth 3

**Ruth 3:1-18 NASB**

**1** Then Naomi her mother-in-law said to her, "My daughter, shall I not seek security for you, that it may be well with you? **2** Now is not Boaz our kinsman, with whose maids you were? Behold, he winnows barley at the threshing floor tonight. **3** Wash yourself therefore, and anoint yourself and put on your best clothes, and go down to the threshing floor; but do not make yourself known to the man until he has finished eating and drinking. **4** It shall be when he lies down, that you shall notice the place where he lies, and you shall go and uncover his feet and lie down; then he will tell you what you shall do." **5** She said to her, "All that you say I will do."

**6** So she went down to the threshing floor and did according to all that her mother-in-law had commanded her. **7** When Boaz had eaten and drunk and his heart was merry, he went to lie down at the end of the heap of grain; and she came secretly, and uncovered his feet and lay down. **8** It happened in the middle of the night that the man was startled and bent forward; and behold, a woman was lying at his feet. **9** He said, "Who are you?" And she answered, "I am Ruth your maid. So spread your covering over your maid, for you are a close relative." **10** Then he said, "May you be blessed of the Lord, my daughter. You have shown your last kindness to be better than the first by not going after young men, whether poor or rich. **11** Now, my daughter, do not fear. I will do for you whatever you ask, for all my people in the city know that you are a woman of excellence. **12** Now it is true I am a close relative; however, there is a relative closer than I. **13** Remain this night, and when morning comes, if he will redeem you, good; let him redeem you. But if he does not wish to redeem you, then I will redeem you, as the Lord lives. Lie down until morning."

**14** So she lay at his feet until morning and rose before one could recognize another; and he said, "Let it not be known that the woman came to the threshing floor." **15** Again he said, "Give me the cloak that is on you and hold it." So she held it, and he measured six measures of barley and laid it on her. Then she went into the city. **16** When she came to her mother-in-law, she said, "How did it go, my daughter?" And she told her all that the man had done for her. **17** She said, "These six measures of barley he gave to me, for he said, 'Do not go to your mother-in-law empty-handed.'" **18** Then she said, "Wait, my daughter, until you know how the matter turns out; for the man will not rest until he has settled it today."

In verse one, Naomi suggests to Ruth that she should look for security for her. When she makes this suggestion, she literally meant a place of rest. Are you looking for a place of rest or are you living in restlessness? In Matthew 11:28-30, Jesus tells us that we can find rest in Him. Jesus is calling. He is calling us to come to Him to find rest, security, and peace for our weary souls. Naomi knows that she cannot provide this rest and security for Ruth because she is old and husbandless. Ruth needs covering, she needs protection, and Naomi sees that Boaz could offer this to Ruth since he was a near relative of her dead husband Elimelech. So she comes up with a plan that had many specifics. Ruth has to go out in secret, anoint herself, put on her best clothes, wait till Boaz was asleep, and then lie at his feet. However, with the Lord, we can come just as we are with all our baggage, doubt, fears, worries and everything else. Jesus is calling us to come and lay it all down at the foot of the cross.

After Ruth works through both harvests for a few months she is now back home with Naomi. From the very beginning Boaz knew who Naomi and Ruth were and he knew he was a kinsman redeemer, but he had not yet decided to act upon his personal responsibilities. I guess Naomi feels that he has had enough time to think about it and to decide whether he wants to bear such a responsibility, so she sends Ruth to him to learn of it. Ruth goes to Boaz in secret during the night. He awakes startled in the middle of the night and asks, "Who is there?" In verse nine Ruth responded, "I am your servant Ruth, spread your garments over me..." My friend we no longer have to sit and hope for redemption or search for it, for we have been redeemed by the blood of the lamb. The moment that we believed that Christ died on the cross and shed His blood for our sins, we became His, and He took our filthy garments and covered us with garments as white as snow. We are now covered with His righteousness. According to Romans 8:1 KJV, "There is therefore now no condemnation to those who are in Christ Jesus."

In verse eleven, Boaz calls Ruth a woman of excellence. Why? Earlier in verse ten he says that she didn't go after young men, whether rich or poor, and she was known as a good person amongst his people. What is your testimony amongst God's people? Yes, you may have a past, but have you actually put it behind you? In 2 Corinthians 5:17 NKJV, the Bible says, "old things have passed away; behold, all things have become new" Have you become new in Christ? God has called you to be a woman/man of excellence regardless of your ethnicity, social status, and family background. You need only believe Him.

In verse fourteen, we read that Ruth gets up early before anyone could recognize her, and Boaz advises that others should not find out that she was there so as to protect her reputation. A woman must know her value and her worth for herself and do what she must to protect it. A woman of excellence should be teamed up with a man of excellence. A man of excellence is a man that loves the Lord and others, and a man that actively seeks to protect a woman's reputation. A man of excellence does not have to be rich, but he should possess these qualities. In verse seventeen, Boaz ensures that Ruth does not go back to her mother-in-law empty handed. He is conscious of the fact that the harvest is over, and they are in need. Maybe he was also thinking about their future needs. He knew that he wanted to redeem them but that the situation might have taken a while to be completely worked out, and so he wanted to make provision for them during the upcoming waiting period. This reminds me so much of Jesus and the Holy Spirit. Jesus had to go back to heaven so that the rest of the redemption story could be played out on earth. He knew that it would take some time before His return, so He sent the Holy Spirit to live within us so that:

1) We won't ever be alone.

2) The Holy Spirit could lead and direct us into all truth.

He made provision for our present and future. So we are not

just sitting and waiting empty handed, we have His Spirit and His word (John 16:13).

In verse eighteen, Naomi tells Ruth to sit and wait, a phrase that no one likes to hear! It is a period of uncertainty. During such periods, one's faith can waiver and doubt and fear can creep in. At such times the enemy likes to come in and tempt us, but it can also be a period where our faith in God can be proven to be true. James 1:2-4 NLT tells us, "consider it an opportunity for great joy. For you know that when your faith is tested, your endurance has a chance to grow. So let it grow for when your endurance is fully developed, you will be perfect and complete, needing nothing." To be honest this is not one of my favourite verses in the Bible. There is no easy way out and no shortcuts. We are simply told to rejoice in the midst of adversity. It isn't about how we feel in the situation. When we don't have good feelings about something, it makes it all the more difficult to be joyful and to have peace. Thank God that we don't have to sit and wait in vain, for our hope is in Him. Hebrews 11:1 NLT says, "faith is the confidence that what we hope for will actually happen, it gives us assurance about things we cannot see." We have confidence in God that He is faithful to complete the good work which He started in us (Philippians 1:6). We can be confident in the fact that just as Boaz did not rest, but immediately attended to the matter Ruth brought to him, Jesus also is not resting, He is fighting for us. I just love the passage in Daniel 10:12-20 which says that even from the first time that Daniel prayed, God heard him. He sent a response, but there was war waging in the heavens. Can you imagine that in these moments as we sit and wait, there are things taking place in the heavenly realms on our behalf? There is a war being waged over our very lives and there is a lot of opposition. God has not forgotten about you and your situation, even though it may seem like you have been sitting and waiting and praying for a very long time! Maybe it's been a few months, a year, or many years. Yes it is difficult to keep the faith and sometimes we grow tired and feel like giving up. But dear one, remember Romans 8:37-38 NLT which says, "No, despite all these things, overwhelming victory is ours through Christ, who loved us. And I am convinced that nothing can ever separate us from God's love…"

**A woman must know for herself her value and her worth and do what she must to protect it.**

# Questions
Ruth 3:1-18

1) Would you consider yourself a woman of excellence?

2) What is your definition of a woman of excellence? Is it biblical?

3) What things can you change about yourself to become a woman of excellence/a woman of promise?

4) Have you ever found yourself in a waiting period?

5) How did you respond? Were you filled with worry and fear or with peace and joy? _____

_____
_____
_____
_____

6) What do your emotions reveal to you about your faith?

_____
_____
_____
_____
_____

7) What do they reveal to you about your belief in God?

_____
_____
_____
_____
_____

8) What steps/choices can you make to strengthen your faith in God?

_____
_____
_____
_____
_____

9) What verses can you meditate on to help you?

_____
_____
_____
_____
_____

10) If you are not yet married, are you desiring a man of excellence or a man of the world? _____
_____
_____
_____
_____

11) List some characteristics of a man of excellence that will help you to recognize him? _____
_____
_____
_____
_____

12) What are some steps that you can take to avoid settling for someone who is not a man of excellence? _____
_____
_____
_____
_____

# Additional Insights

# Additional Insights

# Viewer Guide – Session Six
Ruth 4:1-22

In this session we will focus on God's redemptive plan for Ruth and the world.

The GATE - The gate was used as a place for public _____, assembling of the people, gathering news, having _____.

The kinsman would inherit Ruth, the widow, and be responsible to _____ up the name of the _____ on his inheritance.

LESSON #26 - DO NOT _____ YOUR BLESSING.

This path that you are on is not just a path to _____ for your personal struggles. God wants to do so much more than that. He wants to _____ the entire earth.

JESUS CHRIST came as the _____ Adam so that we can now _____ ETERNAL LIFE.

We are sealed with the HOLY _____ until the day of _____ when we will receive our new RESURRECTION BODIES and our _____! (Ephesians 1:9-140)

LESSON #27 - JESUS WILL _____.

YHWH provided a redeemer for Ruth through _____ and Ruth provided a redeemer for Naomi through _____!

May your TESTIMONY spread the _____ of God.

LESSON #28 - GO (IN FAITH) AND _____ NO MORE. (John 8:11)

# Prayer Points

- Ask the Lord to give you a deeper understanding of your new position in Christ as an heir.

- Ask the Lord to reveal to you the depth of the redemption he has provided for you and the entire world through the death of his son Christ Jesus on the cross.

- Pray for the strength to let go of anything that may be hindering you from walking in faith.

- Pray for your faith to be increased.

- Pray for the courage to find ways to share your testimony with others so that you can bring fame to the name of God.

# Ruth 4

### Ruth 4: 1-22 NASB

**1** Now Boaz went up to the gate and sat down there, and behold, the close relative of whom Boaz spoke was passing by, so he said, "Turn aside, friend, sit down here." And he turned aside and sat down. **2** He took ten men of the elders of the city and said, "Sit down here." So they sat down. **3** Then he said to the closest relative, "Naomi, who has come back from the land of Moab, has to sell the piece of land which belonged to our brother Elimelech. **4** So I thought to inform you, saying, 'Buy it before those who are sitting here, and before the elders of my people. If you will redeem it, redeem it; but if not, tell me that I may know; for there is no one but you to redeem it, and I am after you.'" And he said, "I will redeem it." **5** Then Boaz said, "On the day you buy the field from the hand of Naomi, you must also acquire Ruth the Moabitess, the widow of the deceased, in order to raise up the name of the deceased on his inheritance." **6** The closest relative said, "I cannot redeem it for myself, because I would jeopardize my own inheritance. Redeem it for yourself; you may have my right of redemption, for I cannot redeem it." **7** Now this was the custom in former times in Israel concerning the redemption and the exchange of land to confirm any matter: a man removed his sandal and gave it to another; and this was the manner of attestation in Israel. **8** So the closest relative said to Boaz, "Buy it for yourself." And he removed his sandal. **9** Then Boaz said to the elders and all the people, "You are witnesses today that I have bought from the hand of Naomi all that belonged to Elimelech and all that belonged to Chilion and Mahlon. **10** Moreover, I have acquired Ruth the Moabitess, the widow of Mahlon, to be my wife in order to raise up the name of the deceased on his inheritance, so that the name of the deceased will not be cut off from his brothers or from the court of his birth place; you are witnesses today." **11** All the people who were in the court, and the elders, said, "We are witnesses. May the Lord make the woman who is coming into your home like Rachel and Leah, both of whom built the house of Israel; and may you achieve wealth in Ephrathah and become famous in Bethlehem. **12** Moreover, may your house be like the house of Perez whom Tamar bore to Judah, through the offspring which the Lord will give you by this young woman." **13** So Boaz took Ruth, and she became his wife, and he went in to her. And the Lord enabled her to conceive, and she gave birth to a son. **14** Then the women said to Naomi, "Blessed is the Lord who has not left you without a redeemer today, and may his name become famous in Israel. **15** May he also be to you a restorer of life and a sustainer of your old age; for your daughter-in-law, who loves you and is better to you than seven sons, has given birth to him." **16** Then Naomi took the child and laid him in her lap, and became his nurse. **17** The neighbor women gave him a name, saying, "A son has been born to Naomi!" So they named him Obed. He is the father of Jesse, the father of David. **18** Now these are the generations of Perez: to Perez was born Hezron, **19** and to Hezron was born

Ram, and to Ram, Amminadab, **20** and to Amminadab was born Nahshon, and to Nahshon, Salmon, **21** and to Salmon was born Boaz, and to Boaz, Obed, **22** and to Obed was born Jesse, and to Jesse, David.

As we continue to read in chapter four, we see the fulfillment of hopes and dreams. When God opens a door for you, no man, no demon, nothing in heaven and hell can shut it! God is the only one who can move beyond culture, boundaries, and tradition. God is the one who gives favour and blessings and orchestrates every part of our lives. Can you imagine if Ruth had given birth to a son for her now dead husband? In the midst of her loss and sorrow, God made a better way for her through Boaz. What is even more surprising and blows me away is the blessings that the elders pronounce on Boaz and Ruth. The elders are simply there to be witnesses to the transaction taking place between Boaz and the other man, but instead they pronounce blessings which seem to be very prophetic. Why should they want a Moabitess woman to flourish like Rachel and Leah? The blessings that they pronounce for Boaz seemed quite logical because he is a good man, has a great reputation, and is well known, but Ruth? I suppose that if nothing else because of her association with Boaz—him taking her as his wife, they want her to be as fruitful as possible. This reminds me of our relationship to Jesus Christ. We are so unworthy of any blessings, but because of our association with Him, we are now joint heirs with Him (Romans 8:17). Ephesians 1:3 says that He has blessed us with every spiritual blessing. Can you believe that? There is absolutely no logical reason that we should have and possess the same blessings as Christ, but He has chosen us and given them to us. In verse twelve, we also see that they mention Tamar as well. She was the one who disguised herself as a prostitute and slept with her father-in-law, Judah, because he would not give her another one of his sons to marry. (Judah was the son of Leah, and he is the patriarch of one of the twelve tribes of Israel). Tamar did this so that she could produce an heir for her dead husband. Tamar was almost killed for her act, but in the end she was justified. So the elders hope that Boaz's house will be like the house of Perez, the son of Tamar, through the offspring he will have through Ruth… So many blessings!

I think about what a shame it is that the closest kinsman redeemer didn't redeem Ruth for himself. He lost out on such a wonderful inheritance because he didn't want to risk damaging his already existing inheritance (verse six). The inheritance that he would have had with Ruth would have been so much greater. How many times do we miss out on God's inheritance and blessings for us because we don't want to risk losing/damaging what we already have? We rather secure what we have now, what we can see, the immediate and present instead of stepping out in faith and entrusting it to God. Don't you know that we serve a God who is faithful and able to multiply what we have? He is the God that said "Give and it shall be given unto you; good measure, pressed down, and shaken together and running over" (Luke 6:38 KJV). In Matthew 14:16-18, Jesus was able to take five loaves and two fish and feed over 5,000 people, and there were twelve baskets of leftovers. Where we see limitations, God sees potential and abundance.

Verse thirteen tells us that Boaz marries Ruth and she gives birth to a son. In verse fifteen, the women bless Naomi saying, "May he be one to you who restores life." This is what your relationship with Jesus does. It gives you life and hope. The Bible says in 1 Corinthians 1:18 NLT, "The message of the cross is foolish to those who are headed for destruction. But we who are being saved, know it is the very power of God." Also read Matthew 16:24-25, and so the story comes to an end with Ruth giving birth to her son Obed. Interestingly it is the women, her neighbors, not Naomi or his parents that give him this name. Remember in the beginning of the story

Naomi told them to call her Mara, but now having seen all that the Lord has done for Naomi and Ruth, they find it fit to call the son Worshipper. They believe that God is to be worshipped because of all that He has done for them. Psalm 113:3 says that He is worthy to be praised from the rising of the sun until the going down of the same. Tamar who had stepped out in faith had an impact on future generations. She never knew that Boaz would be born through her lineage and that he would marry Ruth the Moabitess. At the end of the chapter we see that Obed became the father of Jesse. Jesse was the father of David, and David was the ancestor of Jesus Christ. My friend you can never lose when you place your faith in God. He will never fail you. At the end of your journey, may you be able to say like Paul in 2 Timothy 4:7 NLT, "I have fought the good fight, I have finished the race, and I have remained faithful."

# Additional Insights

# Additional Insights

# Additional Insights

# Viewer's Guide Fill in the Blank Answers

## Week 1

Promise Land, Projected Reality, Warnings, Actuality
Lesson #1 Reality, Actuality
Enemies, Ehud
Lesson #2 Playing, Enemy
Ehud, Instability, Famine, Eglon, Eighteen (18)
Lesson #3 Land, Fruitful
Conquered, Lost
Lesson #4 Decisions, Famine
Lesson #5 Listening

## Week 2

Ephrathites, Judah, Fruitfulness, Twelve (12), Tribes.
Bethel, Twenty-two thousand (22,000), Eighteen thousand (18,000), Rimmon.
Lesson #6 Victory, Denial
Lesson #7 Compromise, Compromise
Ehud, Eglon, Famine
Lesson #8 Restore, Dry, Places
Lesson #9 Harden
Lesson #10 Process, Repentance, Intentionality, Work.
Lesson #11 Eliminate.
Lesson #12 Influencing

## Week 3

Lesson #13 Security
Repose, Peaceful, Consolation, Abode
Unstable, Anxiety, Disquiet, Uneasiness
Lesson #14 Words
Lesson #15 Identity
Identity, Security, Identity, Security.
Blood, Redeemer
Help, Rescue
Lesson #16 Watch, Follow

## Week 4

Lesson #17 Humility
Eyes, Field
Lesson #18 Sacrifice
Lesson #19 Evidence
Lesson #20 You Favor
Lesson #21 Persistent

## Week 5

Lesson #22 Strategic
Day, Time, Place, Thing.
Lesson #22.1 Man
Lesson #22.2 Best Time
Lesson #22.3 Prepare
Wash, Anoint, Dress, Go.
Lesson #23 Strategic Counselor
Lesson #24 Approach
Secretly, Quietly
Lesson #25 Sit, Wait

## Week 6

Deliberation, Witnesses
Raise, Deceased
Lesson #26 Forfeit
Redemption, Redeem, First, Inherit, Spirit, Redemption, Inheritance.
Lesson #27 Redeem
Boaz, Obed, Fame
Lesson #28 Sin

# Beloved

She was lost but now she has been found!

Buried in sorrow, dejected and defeated

But she arose from the ashes, clothed

In pearly white - A Woman of Promise

Death couldn't take her

Sin couldn't hold her captive

Words couldn't convince her

Only the Saviour could lead her to Redemption

Come away from your hopelessness, come away my

Beloved, my precious one, for you are a Woman of Promise.

## Leah Joslyn

# About the Author

Leah Joslyn is a native of the twin island of Trinidad and Tobago in the Caribbean.

She has been serving as a full-time missionary in West Africa since 2015 with a focus on church planting amongst ethnic groups.

She has degrees in Biblical Studies, Intercultural Studies and is presently finishing her M.A. in Intercultural Studies.

Leah also speaks several foreign languages which include French and other native languages.

She is passionate about working with women, demonstrating how God's Word can be applied to all areas of life and helping them walk in freedom.

Visit LeahJoslyn.com to learn more.

Connect with the author  @leah.joslyn  |   Leah.Joslyn.

If you enjoyed this book, please leave a review on Amazon, and purchase copies for your loved ones or ministry groups.

# Also Available from the author:

www.ingramcontent.com/pod-product-compliance
Lightning Source LLC
Chambersburg PA
CBHW060031180426
43196CB00044B/2438